OUR TIME AMONG ROSES

Poems by **Allison Joseph**

No Chair Press

Carbondale, IL 62901

Table of Contents

For Robert and for Jon
and for saving myself

Long may our love poems live

Impatient

I want to draw you close
Embrace your daily change
The ordinary life
How schedules rearrange

I want to feel you near
On holidays or nights
When skies are still and clear
A sculpted moon in sight

In pleasure or in pain
I want to see your face
Want memories of your skin
That time cannot erase

In time we'll have our time
Our moments of delight
Impatient I send lines
To keep you in my sight

Cross Country

I hope you find exciting
These words I send to you
You're sparking all this writing
My way to tend to you

I cannot cook you dinner
I can't sneak in your bed
What's left for this dear sinner?
I'll get into your head

With stanzas and with sayings
With cultivated tact
I haven't finished playing
This isn't a last act

More like a new beginning
A start I dare to share
This distance isn't winning
When words are in my lair

Tease

Resplendent with no clothing
Divine without a stitch
My bare awareness growing
I want to share this gift

This lack of inhibition
This honest dialogue
Authentic is my mission
So won't you play along

So kiss this crease, this wrinkle,
These stretch marks, this new scar
You'll get to know my signals
When I take off this bra

I'll slip out of these panties
Who needs such fancy lace
And moving slow, not frantic
We'll both come face to face

Our Time Among Roses

Soon I will be with you
These months have felt like years
Deep sadness but much joy too
You've comforted my fears

The thrill of time together
Has kept me from despair
Our love a kind endeavor
I needed to declare

Kiss me among the roses
And I will kiss you back
The joy of your embraces
Fulfilling what I've lacked

New lovers in a garden
Of rich and vibrant colors
My rigid heart will soften
With time spent as your lover

A Blessing for Travel

A blessing for our travel
All means to get to you
Without you I unraveled
So what's a flight or two

If we can be together
In spirit and in flesh
A delicate endeavor
But we're up to the test

The miles that live between us
No longer in the way
I'll get to hear your genius
You'll get to see me sway

So blessings on our journey
Our steps in love and faith
I'm in a placid hurry
Because you're worth my wait

En Route

I'll travel far to meet you
To have you in my grasp
Just knowing I will greet you
Brings me some peace at last

By train, by plane, by taxi
All means to get to you
My rigid heart relaxing
Directions clear and true

Departing from my sadness
Arriving in your arms
You'll greet me with your largesse
Of patient wit and charm

If time and love are money
You are my currency
I'll travel, cool yet sunny,
These miles will let us be

Airport Song

Delays can't kill my ardor
My will to get to you
This port's not sky nor harbor
But I will play along

And wait, a patient flyer,
An eager customer
Downplaying my desire
For what I'm lusting for:

The pleasures of your body
The wisdom from your lips
The both of us more godly
When we touch hip to hip

Then suddenly I'm boarding
My love soon taking flight
The beauty I've been missing
Will greet me well tonight

Healer in a Hotel Room

I see you there writing
A healer in thought
It's rather exciting
This time that we've bought

To journey together
To love and be loved
What will we discover
Beyond and above

Mere casual moments
Time spent off the grid
Affectionate moments
To stop cruelty's skid

I have my own demons
And you have yours too
Such comfortable heathens
With so much to do

Note to Self

Stop hurting and start healing
Girl get on with your life
You know the pain you're feeling
A widow's afterlife

Girl pull yourself together
And make your husband proud
Remember how he loved you
And spoke your name aloud

Song for a Healer

I'd wanted you to heal me
But I have to heal myself
Still want you to feel me
Not giving up that wealth

I love you and I need you
But need to love my life
So much of my past view
Spent being someone's wife

No longer someone's daughter
No longer someone's spouse
I sing into the rafters
Of my deserted house

And in my darkest hour
I will call out your name
My love for you empowered
By this new lack of shame

Velvet Orchid

I'll be your velvet orchid
A fragrance undenied
Unraveled and quite forward
Both student and new guide

So intimate and daring
I'll carry off this scent
Enlightened by your caring
I'll learn my natural bent

My body's celebration
Embracing its own lust
Of joy in recreation
In hips and lips or bust

Relying on my cunning
I will reach out to you
Our love will keep me running
My faith in men renewed

A Novel Interaction

This novel interaction
This shuffling of words
Proves that our attraction
Is not just seen but heard

First time to work together
Is our love now on trend
The keen eye of forever
Can keep us more than friends

How grand to share your story
To learn to play and print
A romp to ease the worries
A read of sly smart wit

More edits and more choices
Lie straight ahead for us
We'll listen to the voices
Of knowledge that we trust

To Satisfy You

To ask for your devotion
Is asking far too much
So I'll ask for the motion
That leads us both to touch

Tell me when you are ready
When you feel shift and stir
Such speaking keeps me steady
Without it I'm unsure

If you want me uncovered
If you want me at all
The feelings I've discovered
Dependent on your call

I want to learn your signals
But need to hear your prayer
A word   a kiss   your fingers
Will surely leave me bare

Joy Ride

God venerate our bodies
Our flesh and all their tears
Pain is a kind of story
That doesn't dim with years

Our passion may be newer
But everything we are
Is lessening and fewer
A history of scars

Yet I cannot stop yearning
I've been through way too much
To stop all of my learning
My mission to be touched

And glad you stepped forward
To join me on this ride
We'll figure out the proverb
To let you groove inside

Extraordinary (after Fiona Apple)

Be kind to me or mean
It doesn't matter which
I am my own machine
Part angel and part bitch

I'm letting loose the angel
Encouraging the bitch
Aware of bitter dangers
And laughing at the kitsch

We frame all love as action
Such sentimental stuff
My own foolish reactions
When mourning made it rough

To live as fully human
With joy and pain combined
I've living now as rumored
With love in my right mind

Adieu

I'm packing up to leave you
Wish I could stay behind
I want to live and breathe you
Scent lingering in mind

I know that I've been grieving
I know that I've been lost
This leaving isn't leaving
I will not pay a cost

For this abrupt departure
This launching into sky
This lover isn't tortured
By knowing I must fly

We'll have more lissome moments
Of chasing the divine
Avoiding all that torment
Yet still in our right minds

A Penny Upon Departure

A penny for my take off
Good luck found on the ground
The sadness that I shake off
Look up while looking down

I'm thinking off your sweetness
To move me through my days
I want to be a witness
To all your playful ways

I know you cannot heal me
I have that work to do
I'm grateful that you've cheered me
Despite the residue

Of mourning through my mornings
And waking through my nights
Insomnia disarming
When I have you in sight

Coda

Our time among the roses
Our subtle mountain climb
Solutions and neurosis
Discussed on our own time

A joy to see you happy
Old fashioned cold on ice
Your repartee still snappy
With teasing your device

I'll fly away still feeling
The finest alcohol
Though I am fairly reeling
I've had no drinks at all

Farewell until our next kiss
The ground time that we'll need
Keep reaching for your right bliss
And I'll respond with speed

Lovers' Postscript

When life is underwhelming
And work's a needed chore
Remember bodies melding
And kissing on the floors

Of a modest chain hotel
In a sprawling cityscape
You learned my body well
In our devout escapes

When life feels like a void
Not worth a sigh or pout
And you wake up annoyed
And full of petty doubts

Remember that we chose
To gift each other bliss
Despite this life's dull blows
We reached toward happiness

About the Author:

Allison Joseph is the author of many collections of poems, including *Confessions of a Barefaced Woman, Professional Happiness, Lexicon, The Last Human Heart, and Speak and Spell.*

The widow of esteemed poet and editor Jon Tribble, she lives and writes in Carbondale, Illinois, where she is on the creative writing faculty of Southern Illinois University.

About this Book:

This book is the last of a trilogy of chapbooks dedicated to the memory of Jon Tribble and in honor of Robert McDowell. I would like to thank both of these exceptional men for being sources of loving inspiration as I continue to navigate the grieving process. The other books in this trilogy are *Bright Fame* and *Psalm for a Second Meeting.*

Notes on the Poems:

"Our Time Among Roses": inspired by the International Rose Test Garden, Portland, Oregon.
"Velvet Orchid": title references a fragrance by designer Tom Ford.
"Extraordinary": the first stanza of this poem alludes to Fiona Apple's song "Extraordinary Machine," off her 2005 album of the same name.